Daily Devotional for Couples

A Powerful Daily Devotional To Strengthen Your

Relationship With The Infallible Word Of God

Alexis G. Roldan

<u>FREE BONUS MATERIAL</u>

Christian Article Series
30 Articles That Will Enlighten Your Faith In God
(Over $27 Value)

For FREE access, go to:

StraightTalkOnLife.com/ChristianArticles

Table of Contents

Introduction

There is a warped notion of how Christians should portray love and be in love. Unfortunately, most people don't seem to understand this which makes it very hard to be a Christian and be in love in the current world.

You don't have to be part of the confused masses. The truth is, God created man and woman and he created love. Of course, considering how emotions can be misunderstood, he devised ways that would make love not only holy but right. If you're able to follow these ways regardless of the stage you're in as a couple, you're assured of happiness and bliss and above all to be right with your maker.

In this devotional book, you will learn the right way to be in love as a Christian and the proper channels that you should use. In the same light, you will get insightful verses from the holy book that should guide you in your journey of keeping your matrimony holy and living within the confines and the comfort of the most high.

How To Use This Book

As a Christian, you always need to be on the same page with your father in heaven. Every little thing you do should make him happy and reflect his image. This applies even when it comes to Love. Whether it is courtship, engagement or marriage, you will need to make sure it is done to God's high standards. This devotional is designed to help you achieve exactly that. You can achieve more from it if you use it in these steps.

1. Over the next one month, each day will have a topic of focus supported by a verse from the bible. Your intention should be to read the verse, internalize it and regurgitate. It would help if you would try and identify how that particular verse applies to your life. That way, it has more meaning.
2. After the verse, there is a brief interpretation, short story or analogy that helps to make the verse easy to understand and digest. This is a great resource if you need better understanding or in depth

understanding of the day's verse. It also helps you prepare for the next part which is equally important in your daily communion with God.

3. As usual, you will need to ask God for guidance in your marriage as a couple or for the stage that your relationship could be in. Each day has a prayer that has been specially designed with regards to the theme of the day. You can feel free to recite the prayers that have been formulated or, you can easily come up with your own. Better yet, you can recite one in the book and extend it with one of your own.

4. Would you like more verses that expound on the topic of the day? There is a 'Further Reading' section at the end of each devotion. Here, you can find useful verses that are relevant and related to the theme of the day. It is a great feature that will allow you to get more verses that you can read through the rest of the day and get a better understanding of the path that God has for you and your beloved.

Day 1: Characteristics Of Love

"Love is patient, love is kind and is not jealous; love does not brag and is not arrogant." 1 Corinthians 13:4

The modern life and certainly our way of life today have made it hard to clearly define romance or love for that matter. The love between two people (a man and a woman) is suddenly not easy to fathom anymore. People have no idea what they like or love in the other person. We suddenly can't differentiate between infatuation and true love. One thing, however, that everyone seems to forget is that certain situations in life have existed since the beginning of time. The only thing that can make us understand love even in these modern (confusing) times is if we go back to the Holy book.

Before we can even get to your day to day challenges as a couple, the first thing you need to be sure of is that you're actually in love – genuine Christ-like love. 1 Corinthians 13 details what love should be like. It should be all the great things without the jealousy, arrogance and braggadocio.

If what you feel feels a lot like love but is tainted with any of these negative characteristics, there is a fair chance that yours is not true love like God had envisioned. Ultimately, one of these negative traits will pull you apart in due time and cause you to separate.

It is very important that you're sure of what you feel for your partner before you can commit to spending the rest of your life with them. A quick self-assessment of the emotions and feelings that you have for them should help you determine what you feel for them. Ideally, this should help you forge the right way forward. Do not forget that love (and one in Christianity) is not secret. It is put out in public for all to see and rejoice.

Prayer

Lord, today I come before you, I may be a confused soul not sure of what my body or heart is telling me but, your word describes the meaning of love just as the way you love me. Instill in me the discipline to differentiate between true love and the desires of the body to keep me from sinning against you.

Further Reading

"The heart is deceitful above all things, and desperately sick; who can understand it?" Jeremiah 17:9

Day 2: Dating With A Purpose

"For this cause a man shall leave his father and his mother, and shall cleave to his wife; and they shall become one flesh." Genesis 2:24

Dating today is defined as two people being together. Certainly, seeing two people together for even a week or two means they are dating. Dating has definitely been misconstrued and has resulted in chaos rather than true love. An adult involving themselves in romantic relationships with the young is illegal in certain settings yet people still refer to it as dating (at least for those who don't end up serving jail terms).

The dating period during a relationship is a very critical time. It is a time within which you get to know and perhaps start understanding what they are about. However, in the secular realm, dating can be a period used to get to know new people without any real intention.

As a Christian, this should not be your path. God has created a path full of good intentions for you. If he has introduced a person in your life it must be for a reason. Not to say that every person you date will lead to marriage, but the intention should be marriage. It is a serious part of courtship and understanding each other.

Dating with a purpose is important because during this time, you spend a lot of time and effort trying to learn someone. During this time, you should also be praying and fasting with the aim of seeking guidance from God to point you towards the right person and keep you from giving in to the desires of your body.

Prayer

God, help me understand the essence of dating. That I may be able to seek your guidance during this important time of my life and that I may find peace and acceptance in the suitors that you have chosen for me. Help me understand them and their shortcoming and that I may use this opportunity as you have destined it to be.

Further Reading

"The father may decide whether he will give his virgin daughter in marriage" 1 Corinthians 7:36

"And he shall take a wife in her virginity" Leviticus 21:13

Day 3: Two Become One

"And the two will become one flesh. So they are no longer two, but one flesh." Mark 10:8

After a lot of soul searching and prayer, God has directed you to the right partner. You have dated in the right way and introduced yourselves and your intentions towards each other to your parents. What is the next stage?

God is a God of order. He loves strategy and organization and works in the same way. Everything has to be systematic and right. Marriage becomes your next big step. Big step because, unlike courtship where you still had your freedom and your standalone opinion, after marriage, you become one. It is no longer about you but, about us, your care for your partner and they care about you.

It is important to understand the depth of scripture when it says that you become one flesh. Technically, you're to remain as your individual selves but, your behaviour, care and even how you talk is to reflect your better half.

That means that you're not only getting married to your partner but, you're to treat them the same way you would treat yourself. You prioritize them and they do the same for you. This is one of the most vital bible verses that can make your marriage a success. Unfortunately, most couples rarely pay attention to the grave impact that it has if practiced to the letter.

Prayer
Almighty God, you have seen it right in your eyes to bless me with a wife (or husband) and I receive your blessings with my arms wide open. I pray that you will teach me to treat them with compassion, love them unconditionally and through their faults that my marriage will work for the glory of your name.

Further Reading
"Then the Lord God made a woman from the rib he had taken out of the

man, and he brought her to the man. The man said, "This is now the bone of my bones and flesh of my flesh; she shall be called woman for she was taken out of man. That is why a man leaves his father and his mother and is united to his wife and they become one flesh." Genesis 2:22-24

Day 4: Is Your Marriage Ideal?

"Owe no one anything except to love each other, for the one who loves another has fulfilled the law." Romans 13:8

When getting into a holy union with your partner, you're expecting an ideal (perfect) marriage. No quarrels (or very minimal and normal) no arguments and no fights. Usually, our expectations in marriage are the first thing that betrays us.

As much as you have dated your partner for a long time and believe you know their best and worst, after marriage, there are situations that will always get you off guard. The truth is, God wants the perfect marriage for you. But, it does not get there without things being real.

Just like in the analogy of the pot and the kiln, problems in marriage are to you what a kiln is to the pot. You will face problems quite often in your real marriage but, the difference is in how you handle them and find solutions. If you're able to amicably find solutions, then without a doubt your marriage will grow and your bond will strengthen. In the long run, you might even have a shot at having the ideal marriage. However, it takes a lot of work getting a real marriage to the ideal situation.

Prayer

I know that my marriage is not perfect. Neither I'm I. But I pray that you give the courage and wisdom to help us make judgements and find solutions that bring us closer to each other and closer to you and in the process, achieve the ideal marriage that you have always envisioned for us.

Further Reading

"And let us consider how we may spur one another on toward love and good deeds, not giving up meeting together, as some are in the habit of doing, but encouraging one another- and all the more as you see the day approaching." Hebrew 10:24-25

"There are three things that amaze me – no four things that I don't

understand: how an eagle glides through the sky, how a snake slithers on a rock, how a ship navigates the ocean, how a man loves a woman."
Proverbs 30:18-19

Day 5: Communication And Your Marriage

"Let your speech always be gracious, seasoned with salt, so that you may know how you ought to answer each person." Colossians 4:6

One of the things that make relationships so successful is effective and efficient communication. When a relationship is budding, both parties are able to communicate articulately on their likes and dislikes and problems are nipped in the bud as soon as they arise.

Further down in marriage, this type of communication withers and in its place, you have long bouts of silence with little essential communication going. When your partner wrongs you or the other way around, there is no talk to address the issue.

As a result, the anxiety and tension created starts to weigh on the marriage. One of the most effective tools that you should start practicing today is talking. And, not just uttering words but being careful how you convey the message trying as much as possible to be honest and not offending your partner.

As long as each of you understand the lane that you're on and what makes your partner happy, it makes it easier to play your role in the marriage of making your partner happy. Simply put, silence is the beginning of a failing marriage.

As a couple, you should make it your goal today to speak more often, more eloquently and more effectively easily articulating your problems. It does not matter the approach you're going to take. Whether you will sit down for a couple of minutes in a day and discuss how the day has been including any problems you have faced or have erratic talks about the state of affairs in your home, it does not matter as long as you start talking.

Prayer

In your word, you have said that you love the wise, people who can hold their tongues and speak when necessary. Help me become such a person. One who talks with diligence and eloquence and is able to express their feelings with ease. Make this a culture in our marriage that we may be able to honor what you put together and never break apart.

Further Reading

"A soft answer turns away wrath, but a harsh word stirs up anger."
Proverbs 15:1

Day 6: The Role Of Faith In Marriage

"And now these three remain: faith, hope and love. But the greatest of these is love." 1 Corinthians 13:13

Faith in your salvation is very critical. It is one of the pillars of your Christianity and your journey towards eternal life. Being able to believe in what you have not seen or what has not yet happened.

You need to bring your strong faith into your marriage as well. The same way you have faith in God to redeem you from a tough situation is the same way you should have faith in your marriage and in God being able to make it work.

The truth is your love and marriage cannot really work without faith. It is an integral part of a successful marriage. Even when you got married, you did not know for sure that your marriage was going to work. However, you did have faith that it would.

Your faith can be expressed in different ways and you can practice using a variety of avenues. Praying for your partner and supplicating on their behalf is one of the best ways for you to show faith. Even praying to God when your marriage is on the rocks shows a lot of faith. Even in the darkest of times, you have to be able to have hope in the unseen that God will swoop in and redeem you.

However, even when practicing faith, remember that is it best accompanied by action for that faith to be fruitful. You need to do your part as a couple and as an individual for God to do his part.

Prayer
Lord, today you have taught us to carry our faith into our marriage and trust that as you say in your word that your plans for us are nothing but good, you will help us steer our relationship in the right direction and foster and deepen our faith in each other and in you.

Further Reading
"Let love and faithfulness never leave you; bind them around your neck,

write them on the tablet of your heart. Then you will win favour and a good name in the sight of God and Man." Proverbs 3:3-4

Day 7: The Christian Couple And Sex

"Marriage should be honored by all, and the marriage bed be kept pure, for God will judge the adulterer and all the sexually immoral." Hebrews 13: 4

As Christian, God's guidance on sex and how it should be enjoyed is very clear. You're not to commit adultery neither are you to commit fornication. Sex is not a tool for the youth to enjoy themselves. Instead, it is the binding glue of marriage.

Sex in Christianity is not immoral in itself. However, when practiced at the wrong time and with the wrong people, it becomes a sin. God himself ordered man to fill the earth and the only way that would be done is through intercourse.

However, he did set clear guidelines on how you could sanctify sex and not be a sinner by practicing. For starters, he made it clear that sex is only acceptable between a man and his wife. Also, the two should not be related and not of the same sex.

It is important for you to make sure that you stay within these guidelines. Sexual immorality according to 1 Corinthians 6:18 is the only sin that you can commit against your own body and this kind of immorality is constantly rebuked in the bible and by God.

It is important for every couple to understand that sex is not immoral only if it is practiced between the two of them.

Prayer

Oh how you hate sinners Almighty God. Forgive me for any wrong that I might have done knowingly or unknowingly and help me to only engage intimately with my partner in a way that pleases you and avoid defiling myself with any sexual immorality.

Further Reading

"But because of immoralities, each man is to have relations with his own wife and each woman with her own husband. A husband should give to

his wife her sexual rights, and likewise a wife to her husband." 1 Corinthians 7: 2-3

Day 8: The Spice Of Appreciation

"Give thanks in all circumstances; for this is God's will for you in Christ Jesus." 1 Thessalonians 5:18

From a young age, you're taught to say thank you and even your parents try their best to appreciate you for every little thing that you do. Even as a toddler, one of the best tools of motivation is appreciation.

The same should be adopted in marriage. Appreciation shows recognition of the good deeds of your partner. When thanking God for blessing you with a great wife or husband, you should not forget to thank your partner as well.

It might not sound as much but, saying "thank you" occasionally among other magic words like "sorry" can go a long way in making your marriage better and stronger. They are simple words that carry a lot of weight and can lead to great positive changes in the atmosphere and effort that your partner places in serving you.

Even as you bear your own little children, some of the most important lessons that you should teach them at a tender age is the art of appreciation for when you teach them when they are young; they never deviate from them even when they grow up.

It is always a great idea to say thank you whenever something good is done to you. It does not matter whether you have received a bouquet of flowers or breakfast a thank you goes a long way.

Prayer
There are a lot of things that I take for granted. Whether it is the gift of life, your grace in my life or for a great partner, I thank you for everything Lord. Remind me to always be grateful for every little thing I have not only to you but also to my partner for their effort in making me happy and helping me grow spiritually and in ways that please you.

Further Reading
"Be kind to one another, tender-hearted, forgiving one another, as God

in Christ forgave you." Ephesians 4:32

Day 9: A Couple That Prays Together Stays Together

"Again, truly I tell you that if two of you on earth agree about anything they ask for, it will be done for them by my father in heaven. For where two or three gather in my name, There I am with them." Matthew 18:19-20

If you're a Christian, you know how important prayer can be in your journey towards salvation and particularly in your life.

The spirit of prayer should also be exercised in your marriage. It's not enough that you pray alone. Even though that is very important, you should set some time apart where you get to pray together. Remember that you're not considered as one flesh in the eyes of God and those of the church. Supplicating and seeking forgiveness from God together can prove to be very important.

Not only does praying together give you more time to be together, it also gives you a chance to present yourselves before the Lord together and in unison. God's word also says, "Where two or more gather in my name, there I am with them." You can rest assured that he will be there with you as you pray together.

If you have any children, you should also involve them in your prayer sessions. It is a great chance to teach them how to pray and about the good deeds of God. As you will realize, praying together is bonding and supplicating for each other lets you know how much your partner cares for you and that they are aware of the problems that you might be facing in your life.

Prayer
Lord, as I pray for strength and ability to keep my family together, help me teach them the essence of praying together and that my children will grow up knowing and fearing you and working to please you throughout their lives.

Further Reading
"How good and pleasant it is when God's people live together in unity! It

is like precious oil poured on the head, running down the beard, running down on Aaron's beard, down the collar of his robe. It is as if the dew of Hermon were falling on Mount Zion. For there the Lord bestows his blessing, even life forevermore." Psalm 133:1-3

Day 10: Let God Steer Your Marriage

"That people may know, from the rising of the sun and for the west, that there is none besides me; I am the Lord, and there is no other. I form light and create darkness, I make well-being and create calamity, I am the Lord, who does all these things." Isaiah 45:6-7

Sometimes, we forget just how much power God has and how he can change any situation that you might be in. The only problem is in most cases, as much as we need him to redeem us, we don't want to relinquish control and let him takeover.

Even in your marriage, he has a plan. Despite where you want to drive your marriage, you should now that his will is always going to stand.

Your role is to always seek God's guidance in every decision you make for your marriage and in it. If you get this right, chances of you ever going wrong will be very minimal or close to none. The best part is you will always end up making the right decisions not only for your marriage and your partner but also for the bigger plan that God has for you. You should also remember that God says his great plans for are you good and to make you successful and not to harm. Surely, you want to be part of those good plans God has.

It does not matter whether you're in a good or bad situation. It does not even matter how you got there. All that should matter is for you to be willing to let go and let God take the wheel. Let him steer this relationship however and whichever direction he pleases. After all, he is all knowing!

Prayer

I know that as your child I might derail from your plans from time to time. I might forget to let you take the lead and forget that you know what is best for me. Today, I let go entirely. I put my life and marriage in your capable arms for you to show me the exploits that you have in store for me.

Further Reading

"Trust in the Lord with all your heart, and do not lean on your own understanding. In all your ways, acknowledge him, and he will make straight your paths." Proverbs 3:5-6

"For I know the plans that I have for you, declares the Lord, plans for welfare and not for evil, to give you a future and a hope." Jeremiah 29:11

Day 11: Leave The Past Out Of It!

"Who then is the one who condemns? No one. Christ Jesus who died— more than that, who was raised to life—is at the right hand of God and is also interceding for us." Roman 8:34

One of the biggest hurdles to any relationship is baggage from the past. As humans, we don't have the forgiving nature that our father in heaven does. While he is generous and forgives whole heartedly, for us, forgiving and putting the mistake behind us is something that does not come naturally.

How many times have you had a disagreement and in the process brought up an issue from your partner's past. Something that you had already discussed and already settled and forgiven each other about suddenly comes back again.

Not only does this set back the matter at hand, it also sets the relationship back. Learning to forgive and letting the past remain in the past is a critical part of the growth of every relationship. Just as your father forgives you of all your shortcomings and does not hang them around your neck, so should you do not only in your relationship and marriage but also to fellow human beings.

Complete forgiveness is not an easy task but, with practice, it is one that you can perfect. The best part is, forgiving and letting go also sets you free and makes you feel lighter and happier.

Prayer

Thank you God for having forgiven me my sins and having made me a better person and your child. May you give me the humility and a forgiving heart to not only forgive those who do me wrong but also let it go and start a new life. Help to me to always leave the past out of my marriage and concentrate of the bright future that you have for us.

Further Reading

"Get rid of all bitterness, rage and anger, brawling and slander, along with every form of malice. Be kind and compassionate to another,

forgiving each other, just as Christ forgave you." Ephesians 4:31-32.

Day 12: Marriage – A Loving Gift From God

"He who finds a wife finds what is good and receives favour from the Lord." Proverb 18:22

Marriage is inspired by love and a need to find someone to share your life with, start a family and finally get things moving in your next stage in life. Above all, marriage is God's gift to man.

From the book of Genesis when God created woman, he made it clear that woman and man belonged together. At the time, sin had not become part of man and there were no clear guidelines on how the two would engage.

After sinning, God still had the same plan for both but this time, because of sin and sexual immorality, there needed to be a protocol that needed to be followed to make the vows holy and right before God. There came marriage.

God not only applauds a man who finds a good wife. He goes ahead to say, that such a man receives favour in his eyes. That goes to show how highly God regards marriage especially considering that it was his idea.

Prayer
Thank you Lord for the gift of marriage. The ability to say my vows to my wife (or husband) and the grace of being able to keep them this far. I pray for continued strength and passion that I may keep this beautiful relationship going and that I may continue to find favour in your and in the eyes of men.

Further Reading
"Sometimes I wish everyone were single like me – a simpler life in many ways! But celibacy is not for everyone any more than marriage is. God gives the gift of the single to some, the gift of married life to others." 1 Corinthians 7:7

Day 13: Steer Clear Of The Desires Of The Body

"Flee the evil desires of youth and pursue righteousness, faith, love and peace along with those who call on the Lord out of a pure heart." 2 Timothy 2:22

Your only hindrance and perhaps the cradle of sin is your flesh. A human being is comprised of the soul and the flesh. In most cases, as much as we know what is right, the demands of the flesh can be overwhelming which might cause us to sin.

A good Christian is one that not only understands the bible but also one that has mastered the art of self-control and is able to fore go the demands of the flesh.

A great example of how the flesh falters is at the Garden of Gethsemane. While Jesus was praying, his disciples were sleeping. They might have wanted to pray but the demand by the flesh to sleep instead was too much.

It is a tall order for any Christian to tame their worldly desires. However, in due course, it is possible. Spiritual fetes like fasting are quickly dampened by a demanding body. You have to be vigilant and diligent in feeding your spirit more than your flesh if you're going to stay true to the narrow path.

Prayer

Lord, I come before you today with a humble heard and praying for my spirit and flesh. That you might strengthen my spirit and give me the courage and the strength to tame my body that it may not lead me to sin.

Further Reading

"In order that the righteous requirement of the law may be fully met in us, who do not live according to the flesh but according to the spirit." Romans 8:4

Day 14: Seeking A Godly Partner For Marriage

"Every good gift and every perfect gift is from above, and cometh down from the father of lights, with whom is no variableness, neither shadow of turning." James 1:17

From Jacob and Isaac and even Rebekah in the bible, we see that choosing the right partner that will help you achieve your goals in life and in salvation has always been practiced. Back then there were different guidelines that the parents and even the potential suitors used to pick the right wives for themselves.

In our lives today, choosing a partner for marriage should not only be dictated by your emotional feelings towards the person. In many cases, marriage has been the reason why most people have been disconnected from God. It is an unfortunate instance that is highly regrettable.

Considering that marriage is something that God holds very highly, it needs to be the one thing that draws you closer to your creator. The only way you can achieve this purpose is by making sure you choose a Godly partner.

The bible is littered by characteristics of a Godly partner. From fearing the Lord, being upright in your ways, Loving God, being a person of your word, knowing how to control your tongue and yourself and also being a faithful lover.

Other than being a great provider, or being a great cook or house keeper, you should endeavour to make sure that the partner you choose for marriage has all the Godly traits in him or her and that they will also help you grow spiritually.

Prayer

My prayer today is that you lead to a person that will not only make me better but also draw me closer to you and make me a better child and servant to you. May you lead me to a partner who fears you and one who will complete me spiritually.

Further Reading

"An excellent wife is the crown of her husband, but she who shames him is as rottenness in his bones. Proverbs 12:4

Day 15: Marriage Is Holy, Treat It As Such

"Give honor to marriage and remain faithful to one another in marriage. God will surely judge people who are immoral and those who commit adultery." Hebrews 13:4

Couples rarely understand how seriously God takes marriage. Take a moment and think of what it took for some of the greatest men in the Bible to gain favour from God. A lifetime of commitment to salvation and constantly seeking Holiness.

Yet, in his word he says, that he who finds a good wife obtains favour from God. Eternal life and salvation are all free. But God does not make them as easy as reach out and grab. You have to work. Marriage is one of the ways but only when it is done right.

To make sure that you're not confused in the process, God has set rules that should drive any marriage that is pleasing in his eyes. One of these is that you shall not divorce unless in cases of adultery.

He proceeds to emphasis on the importance of love among couples, the qualities of a good wife and a good husband (who should be a provider to his family) and so forth. Each of these factors contributes to making a marriage less challenging and if followed to the letter, it could be a very happy and harmonious life.

Prayer

Lord, we thank you for our marriage and for the far that you have brought us. We thank you today for reminding us of how holy and highly you regard marriage and it is our prayer that every waking day, we will be able to follow your guidelines on having a successful marriage and staying together as that is what makes you happy.

Further Reading

"At the beginning, God made them male and female. For this reason a man will leave his father and mother and be united to his wife and the two will become one flesh. So they are no longer two but one. Therefore what God has joined together let no one separate." Mark 10:6-9

Day 16: Love One Another

"A new command I give you: Love one another. As I have loved you, so you must love one another." John 13:34

From the beginning, God has been very consistent on the essence of love. From loving yourself, loving your neighbour and even loving your enemy. If there is one thing that makes a marriage work, it is love and without a doubt, it is the same thing that brought you together.

There are different kinds of love and you will need sufficient amounts of each to make your marriage work. Love will go a long way especially when your marriage is facing difficulties.

In case you doubt how much love you should give, God – again gives a very good example. It should be unconditional like his love for his people. Your love should renew each day. With love in your hearts, finding faults in your partner will be a thing of the past. This makes it easier for you to co-exist.

Prayer
Just as we love you Lord and love serving you, may love each other every day of our lives and may our well of love never dry up. May we also love our children, neighbours and even those that do not wish the best for us for your word says that Love is your greatest commandment.

Further Reading
"Be devoted to one another in love. Honor one another above yourselves" Romans 12:10

"Love fulfils the law. Let no debt remain outstanding, except the continuing debt to love one another, foe whoever loves has fulfilled the law." Romans 13:8

Day 17: Remember Holiness And Purity

"But just as he who called you is holy, so be holy in all you do; for it is written: "Be holy for I am Holy." 1 Peter 1:15-16

In your pursuit for happiness even in marriage, you should always remember that your main goal as a Christian and as a child of God is to live a life that pleases the father.

Marriage should not be a reason for you to derail from the path of the greater calling. It is why you have to choose a partner that gives you the urge to continue pursuing Christ with even more vigour. After all, the two of you together should comfort each other in times of difficulty and always be a constant reminder to each other of the love that Christ has for you and the great gift that awaits you if you live your life in accordance to the will of God.

The institution of marriage is pure and holy and after you have tied knot, you vow to keep it as such. You should not let sin creep in or give the devil a chance. With marriage, you have a new challenge which is to not only be the child of God but keep his institution Holy and pure.

The bible has multiple guidelines on keeping your matrimonial bed pure. You should not commit adultery, being faithful and trustworthy and not separating are just some of the few that particular emphasis has been placed upon.

Prayer
Today, your word reminds me to be holy as you have been holy. Even though we are only humans who are prone to error, may your grace and love always bring us back when we veer of your path and may we always remember to keep our matrimony holy and pure.

Further Reading
"Let marriage be held in honor among all, and let the marriage bed be undefiled, for God will judge the sexually immoral and adulterous."
Hebrews 13:4

Day 18: Respect Each Other

"However, let each one of you love his wife as himself, and let the wife see that she respects her husband." Ephesians 5:3

There are two basic principles to a successful marriage. The first is love and the other is respect. Even without looking at the bible to verify this.

Love cannot exist without respect and vice versa. It is imperative for you as a Christian to have love and respect in your heart. Each of these two principles is two-way traffic. For you to receive you have to give.

One thing that God makes very clear is that marriage is not a play toy. You're in it to win it and for the long term. That said, you need to arm yourself with all the ingredients and the tools that will make your marriage successful. One of these is respect. And, this is not only to the wife. Even though emphasis is placed on the wife to respect the husband as the head of the house, the husband also has a role of respecting the wife as a helper.

Prayer
Love and respect are going to take our marriage a long way and your word places emphasis on this. Help us to always remember to treat each other and other people with kindness and respect to forge strong bonds and relationships that never break.

Further Reading
"So in everything, do to others what you would have them do to you, for this sums up the law and the prophets." Matthew 7:12

Day 19: Find Time For Spiritual Growth

"So that Christ may dwell in your hearts through faith; and that you, being rooted and grounded in love, may be able to comprehend with all the saints what is the breadth and length and height and depth, and to know the love of Christ which surpasses knowledge, that you may be filled up to all the fullness of God." Ephesians 3:17-19

As a Christian, your lifetime goal is grow spiritually closer and closer to God and being able to understand what he wants. It is one of the best ways to grow your communication channels with God.

As a couple, this achievement should not change. As much as you're trying to grow in each other, grow your love and extend your marriage, you should never lose focus on the most important thing – growing spiritually.

Growing together in Christ means that you're not only fulfilling your will through your marriage but also through how you live your lives and making sure that everything that you do pleases him. A good example of couples in the bible that continued to grow spiritual despite marriage were Abraham and Sarah and another great example is Eli and his wife Hannah. Marriage is meant to bring you closer to God and to his plans. Not draw you away. From each other, seek passion and motivation to grow together in Christ in your times of joy as much as your times of turbulence.

Prayer

Lord, you created us as your children. Even though we have grown and become of age and now married, we pray that you will always remind us that before we are husbands and wives, we are your children and our priority should be to seek your face as long as we live.

Further Reading

"Like newborn babies, long for the pure milk of the word, so that by it you may grow in respect to salvation." 1 Peter 2:2

Day 20: Traits Of True love (Part I)

"Having your conduct honorable among the Gentiles, that when they speak against you as evildoers, they may by your good conduct which they observe glorify God in the day of visitation." 1 Peter 2:12

Love is an ambiguous word. It is a feeling that is indescribable and hard to define. However, there are certain characteristics that distinguish love from other often confused feelings like infatuation. As a Christian, it is your duty to understand true love so that you might be able to identify it when the Lord presents it to you.

We will break this into three different parts each covered over the next three days. Today, we will discuss one of the most important traits of true love and that is kindness. As far as you're relating to others and especially to your partner, being kind, treating them in a gentle and thoughtful manner goes along way. It goes without mentioning that kindness is also one of the fruits of the Holy Spirit.

Prayer
Lord cultivate in me a kind heart. That I may touch those that I relate with in my actions and in how I speak. That I may be able to treat my spouse in a way that is pleasing to you and to them.

Further Reading
"Who is wise and understanding among you? Let him show by good conduct that his works are done in the meekness of wisdom." James 3:13

Day 21: Traits Of True love (Part II)

"A tranquil heart gives life to the flesh, but envy makes the bones rot."
Proverbs 14:30

True love is not envious

As a Christian, the first thing that you should understand is that you are not of the world. You're just a passer-by. By understanding that, you know that instead of being envious and covetous of the successes of your spouse or even your neighbour, you're happy for them. You rejoice with them.

There are a lot of meanings that are carried with the term envious. It is not only limited to success but it also extends to items and above all people. And to understand the gravity of how wrong envy is, God even has a commandment for it (thou shall not covet your neighbour's wife) it is this envy that drives us to lust.

Your love should not be envious. You should be content with everything that God has given you including your partner fully understanding that you're not of this world and that you're just passing by.

Prayer

Being your child, I know that my home is in heaven. That I am merely a traveller in this world. Thank you for the blessings that you have bestowed upon me and those that you're about to and always remember that I should be envious for my father in heaven is the creator of everything.

Further Reading

"You are still worldly. For since there is jealousy and quarrelling among you, are you not worldly are you not acting like mere humans? 1 Corinthians 10:13

Day 22: Traits Of True Love (Part III)

"Love is patient and kind; love does not envy or boast; it is not arrogant or rude. It does not insist on its own way; it is not irritable or resentful; it does not rejoice at wrongdoing, but rejoices with the truth. Love bears all things believes all things and hopes all things, endures all things." 1 Corinthians 12:4-8

True Love is not boastful and does not parade itself

On the last part of the three-part series on love and what it is all about, we cover one of the biggest misconceptions about love. Publicity and pride!

Love does not brag. It is humble and graceful, thoughtful of others and kind to those that are in need. The bible says, "Humble yourself under the mighty hand of God that he may exalt you."

It is important to remember that the love you're boasting and being proud about is not actually out of your own creation. It is a blessing that has been given to you by God. And, he can also take it away.

Even with greater blessings than love, you need to remain humble and thankful to the almighty for looking down on you with favour. You should not use the blessings that God has given you to become a disgrace to him.

Prayer
You have taught me the ways of your love. Your description of love and how your love for us is like. May we be able to replicate the same signs and characteristics of love time and time again much to the glory of your name.

Further Reading
"For the entire law is fulfilled by keeping one command. "Love your neighbour as yourself. If you bite and devour each other, watch out or you will be destroyed by each other." Galatians 5:14-15

Day 23: Grow Closer To God Not Closer To Sin

"Whoever dwells in the shelter of the most high will rest in the shadow of the almighty. I will say of the Lord," He is my refuge and my fortress, my God, in whom I trust." Psalm 91:1-2

The hard truth is Marriage is an earthly vessel that is meant to teach you to love. That is why it is stated that until death do you apart. However, your relationship with God is eternal.

With that said, marriage should not be the reason for you to drift away from God. Instead, it is meant to bring you closer. Marriage is a sign of the commitment that Jesus has for the church and there is nothing that God wants more than us to learn to love him as opposed to fearing him.

The intimacy that you share in your marriage should rekindle your intimacy with God and help you build a stronger prayer life. Learn to build unity between yourselves and let it be the mirror that points out the flaws in you.

Prayer

Marriage is a great blessing that you have brought into my life. Teach me to use it as a vessel of getting closer to you and to my spouse and to love others unconditionally so using my earthly relationship, I can forge a better eternal one with you God.

Further Reading

"And this is my prayer: that your love may be abound more and more in the knowledge and depth of insight, so that you may be able to discern what is best and may be pure and blameless until the day of Christ, filled with the fruit of righteousness that comes through Jesus Christ- go the glory and praise of God." Philippians 1:9-11

Day 24: Honor Your Marriage

"Marriage should be honored by all and the marriage bed kept pure, for God will judge the adulterer and all the sexually immoral." Hebrew 13:4

The emphasis is on the first part of this verse – marriage should be honored by all. Simply put, a bible verse can't clearer than that.

It is not only you who is meant to honor your marriage but also those around you. Your parents, your friends and even your church members.

It is forbidden for anyone to sleep with a married person let alone a divorced one. It is not biblically correct. However, for others to honor what God has made pure and holy, it has to start with you and your spouse. If you hold yourselves and your marriage with honor then everyone else will.

Prayer

God, cultivate in us a culture of honor. That when our friends and relatives see us, we are clothed in your honor and grace. Help us stretch the same honor to our marriage that we may be an example to others of the great things that you can do for a couple that takes their marriage seriously and are dedicated to living within your guidelines.

Further Reading

"Or do you not know that your body is a temple of the Holy Spirit who is in you, whom you have from God, and that you are not your own? For you been bought with a price: therefore glorify God in your body." 1 Corinthians 6:19-20

Day 25: Keep God At The Center Of Your Relationship.

"We have not ceased to pray for you and to ask that you might be filled with the knowledge of his will in all spiritual wisdom and understanding." Colossians 1:9

Every relationship needs grounding. Other than letting God steer it wherever he pleases, your relationship no matter the stage should be centred around God. He should be the common denominator between the couple.

Having your relationship centred around God means that both of you have the same spiritual goal and direction and that both of your understand that above everything else, you're serving the Lord. It is very important for every relationship both old and young to have direction and to understand priorities.

One of the most important things to note as a young Christian in a relationship is that your relationship with God is the most important. If you find yourself in a situation that does not bring you closer to God, it's better to leave than to lose your Connection with your creator.

Prayer
Knowing that you're the creator of everything and the one that has seen me this far, I want to know you more and more and learn to love and live in your ways. Let me know the essence of having you at the centre of my relationship and marriage and letting you be the anchor that steadies our ship even when the waters get wild.

Further Reading
"For every house is built by someone, but the builder of all things is God." Hebrews 3:4

Day 26: Pursue God Above Everything Else

"Everything is from him and by him and for him. Glory belongs to him forever! Amen!" Romans 11:36

We should always remember that whatever it is that we seek, our father owns it. Whether we are looking for a spouse, wealth, forgiveness or even simple worldly materials like a car, we should always remember who has the power to grant your needs.

The bible says if it is an arm that is going to cause you to sin, you should cut it. The same is true for marriage. It should not be reason for you to sin or go against the will of God. Paul says in Corinthians, he is content being single. It allows him to serve Christ better.

Even though marriage is a blessing and highly acknowledged by God, it should not be the reason you deviate from him. Remember that before anything else, your first and only goal should be to pursue the Lord.

Prayer
I have been brought up in your ways. Learning how to serve you and constantly growing in my journey to salvation. Let no one not even my marriage derail me from my quest of wanting to know you more every day.

Further Reading
"But seek first his kingdom and his righteousness, and all these things will be given to you as well." Matthew *6:33*

Day 27: Take It Day By Day

"So do not worry about tomorrow; for tomorrow will worry about itself. Each day has enough troubles of its own."

It is always good to have a plan for your life. But sometimes and especially with a marriage, it can be overwhelming thinking about what tomorrow will bring when today has so many problems.

In marriage, you don't really need to think about the future. Your father in heaven is worrying about that. Think of today and live for today. Take the blessings that come your way today and make them work for today.

This will also work in your day to day life. Sometimes, bundling the problems that you're likely to face over the next year makes it so hard for you to see the trickles of blessings that come your way on a daily basis. It makes you forget to thank you and increases your chances of questioning God.

Today, change your approach. Think about today and what it holds for you. Through the day, think of the things that could have gone wrong but did not. Be thankful and appreciative for every little thing. Your father in heaven loves a thankful heart.

Prayer

Even though I am faced by problems the size of mountains, I thank you God for the gift of life and a spouse that makes me laugh every morning. I thank you for my health and my relatives. May be appreciative for the little things that you do for me on a daily basis and learn to tackle my problems one day at a time.

Further Reading

"Teach us to number each of our days so that we may grow in wisdom."
Psalm 90:12

Day 28: Give Thanks Every Day

"I will give thanks to you, Lord, with all my heart; I will tell of all your wonderful deeds." Psalm 9:1

You have a beautiful home, beautiful children and a God-sent spouse. When was the last time you knelt down in prayer to say nothing but appreciate God for everything he has done for you that is good?

Chances are, you take about a minute to thank God for life then proceed with your supplication. As important as it is to come to the Lord with all your pains and burdens, it is also very good to remember to say thank you and sing of the wonders that he has done for you.

Most are times when we kneel each day praying to God to help us with a problem but rarely do we remember to say thank your after our problem goes away.

Prayer
Lord, today I come to you to say nothing but thank you. Thank you for the gift of life, for the people who love me, for sending your son to die for me and above all for today's scripture which reminds me to be grateful for all that you have done for me.

Further Reading
"Let them give thanks to the Lord for his unfailing love and his wonderful deeds for mankind." Psalm 107:8-9

Day29: Be A Person Of Honor And Keep Your Word

"When a man makes a vow to the Lord or takes an oath to obligate himself by a pledge, he must not break his word but must do everything he said." Numbers 30:2

In the bible, you come to know God as one to keep his word. Even though it might take years, God never fails to keep a promise. He promised he would deliver the Israelites and he did he gave Abraham a son at a relatively old age and was with Moses as he was leading the Israelites.

Your aim is to always be like God. Which is what makes it very essential for you to be able to keep your promises and honor your word. Even when marrying your spouse, you recited your vows and promised to stay together and nothing will separate you until death.

Despite their profound meaning, these words aren't taken seriously enough. Your word at the alter in the eyes of God and other witnesses, you make a solemn vow to keep working on your marriage through thick and thin.

These vows are recited by both the man and the wife and it is imperative that both of them are able to keep their words. It goes beyond that. Sometimes, when praying, we always tell God that if he blesses us say with a Job or a child, we will give something back to him.

There are very few people that actually remember to even say thank you. God is a caring God and in most cases, he will not take what he has blessed you with away. Nonetheless, such actions dent your credibility as a Christian.

Prayer

God being a man, I am prone to error and forgetfulness. But I pray that every promise and pledge and make whether to you, my wife or fellow men, I will honor so I may be able to replicate your ways and grow closer to you.

Further Reading

"Just say a simple, 'yes, I will' or, 'No, I won't.' Anything beyond that is from the evil one." Matthew 5:37.

Day 30: Grow In Love Each And Every Day

"May the Lord make your love increase and overflow for each other and everyone else, just as ours does for you." 1 Thessalonians 3:12

Our God is an amazing God. A master planner who thinks through everything. Even though marriage is an earthly thing that ends after we die, God has found very impressive ways of making marriage work especially as a tool of teaching.

Marriage is supposed to teach us how to love as unconditionally as God does. That is why God holds it so highly. Of course, unconditional love is not something that you can develop in one day.

You need to start somewhere and constantly grow in love as you grow spiritually. The two need to grow in tandem as opposed to one leaving the other behind. That is the only way you can achieve love just as God has envisioned it in the bible.

Prayer

Even though I have loved with my whole heart, expand my boundaries that I may love more with each passing day. That I may be closer to you and love people and my partner the same way that you have loved me.

Further Reading

"And this is my prayer: that your love may abound more and more in knowledge and depth of insight." Philippians 1:9

Conclusion

Committing your relationship and certainly partnership to the Almighty is definitely the right way to finding happiness for couples. Life can be unstable and quarrels can bring down even the best and strong relationships. When that happens, there is only one way to go-the Bible. Find out what God says about love and staying together as two people meant for each other. The Christian love is not the same as the fairy-tale love. Things do not imaginarily fall into place when two people come together to share their lives with each other. It's a journey that is long and tiresome. As a Christian, the best way to ensure the journey is successful is by involving God in it. Letting Him be the lead every step of the way. A couple that prays together always stays together. Pray every day that your relationship may benefit each of you and above all glorify God.

Before you go, would you please do me a favor? As an Independent Author and Self-Publisher, I don't have a large publishing company promoting my books. What I do have though, are reviews from readers like you. In fact, reviews are the single most important way for me to be able to get in front of more readers. Without them, I have no chance in competing with the larger, more established authors.

With that said, would you please go back and leave an honest review for this book? I would sincerely appreciate it.

Made in the USA
Monee, IL
03 November 2022

17030967R00030